A New True Book

MOOSE

By David Petersen

CHILDRENS PRESS®
CHICAGO

A female moose

PHOTO CREDITS
© Erwin & Peggy Bauer–9, 17, 18, 32, 38
The Bettmann Archive–21
© Reinhard Brucker–13; Field Museum, Chicago, 42, 42 (inset)
Photri–© Leonard Lee Rue III, 16
Root Resources–© Kenneth W. Fink, 11; © Diana Stratton, 23, 35
Tom Stack & Associates–© Diana Stratton, 34; © Wendy Shattil/Bob Rozinski, 36
Tony Stone Images–© Bill Ivy, 2, 15; © Leonard Lee Rue III, 10 (bottom); © Tom Ulrich, 31, 44
SuperStock International, Inc.–© John W. Warden, 8 (bottom)
Valan–© Joseph R. Pearce, Cover, 39; © Stephen J. Krasemann, 7, 25, 27, 28, 45; © Aubrey Lang, 8 (top); © Wayne Lankinen, 10 (top); © Dennis W. Schmidt, 19; © Bob Gurr, 43
Visuals Unlimited–© Glenn M. Oliver, 4; © Rod Kieft/Nature's Bounty, 12; © Will Troyer, 14; © Tom Ulrich, 41

COVER: Bull moose
(early summer antler growth, eating lilypad)

Project Editor: Fran Dyra
Design: Margrit Fiddle

Library of Congress Cataloging-in-Publication Data

Petersen, David.
    Moose / by David Petersen.
        p.   cm.–(A New true book)
    Includes index.
    ISBN 0-516-01069-7
    1. Moose–Juvenile literature.   [1. Moose.]
I. Title.
QL737.U55P485   1994
599.73'.57–dc20
                                            94-10948
                                            CIP
                                            AC

TABLE OF CONTENTS

WHAT IS A MOOSE?

Here's a riddle for you: What's as tall as a basketball player, as long as a small car, as heavy as a horse, loves snow, spends lots of time in the water, has a bell hanging from its neck, and spears and shields growing out of its head?

Whatever it is, it's BIG. As big as . . . a moose!

Weighing up to 1,400 pounds (635 kilograms) or more, the moose is the giant of the deer family. A male Alaskan moose may stand 7 feet (2 meters) high at the shoulders. And it stretches up to 10 feet (3 meters) from its big nose to its stubby tail.

That's a *lot* of moose!

A male Alaskan moose

The bison (above) and the Alaskan brown bear (below)
are the largest wild animals in North America.

The moose is larger than any other member of the deer family.

The moose is the third largest wild animal in North America. Only the bison, or buffalo, and some Alaskan brown bears weigh more than the Alaskan moose.

9

Elk (above) and caribou (below) are other members
of the deer family that live in North America.

In spite of its great size, the moose has a lot in common with its smaller relatives. The other members of the deer family are elk, caribou, and deer.

The white-tailed deer is found in many areas of the United States.

To begin with, all male
deer, including moose,
have bony, treelike growths
on their heads. These are
called antlers.

And moose, like all deer, are ruminants. Ruminants have stomachs with four separate pouches. Deer need this extra stomach power to digest twigs, brush, and grass.

Finally, all deer, including moose, have split, or two-toed, hooves.

A moose's hooves are split into two toes.

But the moose is the
only deer that comes with
a built-in "bell." The bell is
a large flap of skin that
hangs from the moose's
neck.

A mother moose with twin calves. A moose may have one or two calves. Triplets are rare.

The moose has a darker coat than other deer. Baby moose, or calves, are reddish brown.

Moose "language" includes

Moose live far away from cities and other human settlements.

grunts, bellows, bawls,
and the sheep-like bleats
of the calves.

Moose live in some of
the most remote places on
Earth. Very few people ever
see a moose in the wild.

16

SPECIAL NEEDS

The twigs of willow trees are one of the moose's favorite foods.

Only a few wild regions meet the moose's special needs. For example, moose need foods that grow only in the northern forests of America, Europe, and Asia. Favorite moose foods include willow, alder, berry

Moose wade in water to eat aquatic
plants in the summer.

brush, and young trees. During summer, they enjoy aquatic plants such as water lilies.

In winter, moose need snow. They get some shelter from the bitter wind and

Moose stay warm by bedding down in deep snow.

cold by bedding, or lying down, in deep, soft snow.

In their thick fur coats and snow beds, moose can survive winter nights as cold as minus 70 degrees Fahrenheit (minus 57 degrees Celsius).

MOOSE THEN AND NOW

Before Europeans came to North America, moose were far more numerous than they are today.

For centuries, moose meat was an important food for the Native Americans who lived in the northern woodlands. These hunters used bows and arrows. And they never killed more moose than they needed for food.

Native Americans hunted moose in the water.
They could spear the swimming moose from their canoes.

When white settlers
arrived, they too hunted
moose for their meat. But
the settlers used guns,
and they killed many more
moose than the Native
Americans ever had.

Even worse for the moose, the settlers' farms took over much of their habitat. As more and more immigrants came to America, more and more moose lost their homes or their lives.

Today, moose are still plentiful in Alaska and Canada, where the human population is low. But in the lower forty-eight states, moose survive only in the far northern areas. They are still found in states from Maine to North Dakota,

Moose in Grand Teton National Park, Wyoming

and in the Rocky Mountains
as far south as Colorado.

In all of North America
today, there are only about
one million moose. But where
humans have left enough
room, moose continue to
enjoy a wild, free life.

MOOSE CALVES

Moose calves are born in May and June each year. At birth, the calves weigh only 25 to 35 pounds (11 to 16 kilograms). Until they grow big enough to run with their mothers, moose calves are easy prey.

Moose mothers—called cows—must protect their young from wolves, bears, and other predators. They hide their infant calves in thick brush.

Calves stay near their mothers for protection.

Moose don't have very good eyesight. But their hearing and their sense of smell are excellent. This makes it hard for any predator to surprise a watchful mother moose.

If an enemy comes too near her hidden calf, the mother moose puts up a brave fight. Rearing up on her hind legs like a horse, the cow kicks at the attacker with her sharp front hooves.

In this way, moose cows

A nursing calf. The mother's rich milk helps the calf to grow quickly.

often drive off wolves and even grizzly bears.

Moose calves feed on their mother's milk for several months. But soon they also eat grass and other plants. After just five

Baby moose soon learn to eat grasses and other plants.

months, a "baby" Alaskan moose weighs almost 400 pounds (181 kilograms).

By the end of its first summer, the calf eats an adult diet of twigs and other vegetation. (The Algonquian word for moose is *musee*, meaning "twig eater.")

THE MIRACLE OF ANTLERS

Antlers are the treelike "spears" that grow on the heads of all male deer.

Unlike the horns of cattle and goats, deer antlers are made of solid bone. Also unlike horns, antlers sprout, grow, and drop off each year.

Alaskan moose have the largest antlers. They spread as wide as 6 feet 8 inches (2 meters), and weigh up to 90 pounds (41 kilograms).

The antlers of most deer—such as mule deer and elk—are rounded and slender. But moose antlers are broad and flat. They look like big shields. Long, spearlike points called tines stick out from the edges of the shields.

New antlers grow during spring and summer. They are covered with a fuzzy skin called velvet.

An Alaskan
bull moose
with its antlers
covered in
velvet

The velvet encloses
blood vessels that feed
the growing antlers. It also
protects the tender young
antlers against injury.

When the antlers harden
in late August, the velvet

When the antlers are fully grown, the velvet
dries up and comes off in strips and shreds.

dries up and peels off. To
speed this itchy process,
bull moose rub their
antlers on trees and brush.
  When their antlers are
fully grown, the moose are
ready for the mating season.

THE MATING SEASON

Biologists believe antlers are symbols of a male's strength. Every year, between November and December, only the most powerful bulls mate with the cows. This ensures that the next generation of moose will be strong and healthy.

Usually, the biggest and strongest bull moose have the largest antlers.

Usually, the bull moose with the biggest antlers
wins the right to mate with the female moose.

Sometimes, bull moose
fight to the death to see
which one will mate. But
most often, two competing
bulls simply compare
antlers. The smaller-
antlered bull then leaves
peacefully, knowing he
could not win the fight.

Very young bulls have small antlers, but they grow back larger each year.

After the mating season, male moose shed their antlers. In the spring, their new antlers start to grow again.

Until a moose is too old to mate, each year's antlers are larger and more beautiful than the last.

MOOSE ON THE LOOSE

Except for cows with calves, most moose live by themselves.

Unlike elk and caribou, moose do not roam over wide areas. A moose generally spends its entire life within a few small seasonal ranges, rarely larger than a few square miles.

Sometimes, though, young bulls travel hundreds of miles, searching for mates and territories of their own.

In winter, moose seek out ranges that offer deep snow, as well as brush, twigs, and other foods.

Moose can survive very harsh winters in the far north.

A moose wades in a pond in Ontario, Canada.

In summer, moose prefer wet, marshy areas near rivers and lakes. They like to wade in deep water, enjoying the aquatic plants and avoiding biting insects.

If they can find the food, water, and shelter that all wild animals need, moose live to be 12 to 15 years old.

Even in death, the moose is an important part of the northern forest ecosystem. Its flesh feeds bears, wolves, coyotes,

The gray wolf is one of the moose's predators.

eagles, ravens, people,
and other meat eaters.
Its warm hair lines the
nests of birds and small
mammals. Its tough hide

Native Americans used moose hide to make clothing like this shirt. The moccasins (inset) are embroidered with moose hair.

makes fine moccasins and warm clothing. And its bones and antlers provide important minerals for mice and other rodents.

It is best to enjoy moose from a distance.

MOOSE MANNERS

If you ever see a moose in the wild, don't get too close. Cows with calves are edgy—and dangerous.

And bulls are always cranky.

Anyway, who wants to argue with an animal as tall as a basketball player, as long as a small car, as heavy as a horse, with spears and shields growing out of its head?

WORDS YOU SHOULD KNOW

Algonquian (al • GONG • kwee • in) – a group of languages spoken by some Native Americans

antlers (ANT • lerz) – branched, bony growths on the head of an animal in the deer family

aquatic (ah • KWAH • tik) – living or growing in or near water

bell (BEHL) – a large pendant of skin that hangs from the neck of moose and some cattle; also called a dewlap

biologist (by • AHL • ih • gist) – a scientist who studies living things

blood vessels (BLUD VESS • ilz) – tubes that carry blood through the body

ecosystem (EE • koh • SISS • tim) – all the living things in a certain area

generation (jen • er • RAY • shun) – all the individuals born at about the same time

habitat (HAB • ih • tat) – home; a place where an animal can find everything it needs to live

mammal (MAM • il) – an animal that usually has fur, gives birth to live young, and nurses its young on mother's milk

minerals (MIN • er • rilz) – substances such as iron or calcium that are needed in small amounts by living things

range (RAYNJE) – the region in which a plant or animal can be found in the wild

remote (rih • MOHT) – distant; far away from cities or other human settlements

rodent (ROH • dint) – a mammal that has long, sharp front teeth for gnawing

ruminant (ROO • mih • nint) – having a stomach that is divided into four parts

settlers (SET • lerz) – people who come to a new country and establish farms or other homes there

survive (ser • VYVE)—to last; to remain alive after great danger or trouble
territory (TAIR • ih • tor • ee)—an area with definite boundaries that an animal lives in
tine (TYNE)—a long, pointed antler prong
velvet (VEL • vit)—a fuzzy layer of skin that protects and nourishes developing antlers

INDEX

About the Author

David Petersen has watched moose—from a safe and respectful distance—in Alaska, Canada, Montana, Wyoming, and his home state of Colorado. He is the author of Racks: The Natural History of Antlers and the Animals That Wear Them (Capra, 1991) and other natural history studies.